The Free Trade Trap

By
L. T. Reeves, Ph.D.
Professor Emeritus, Samford University

Bookman LLC
Publishing & Marketing

Providing Quality, Professional
Author Services

www.bookmanmarketing.com

ISBN: 1-59453-616-3

Dedicated to

WILLIAM R. BENNETT, Ph.D.

Former Teaching Colleague and Writing Collaborator

Good Friend of Long Standing

Acknowledgments

My very special thanks go to my wife, Sarah Garrett Reeves, for her excellent research and editorial assistance, as well as her encouragement and forbearance throughout the research and writing process.

For their valuable assistance I wish to thank Jean Thomason, Director of the Samford University Library, and Cheryl Cecil, Interlibrary Loan and Resource Retrieval Assistant, Reference Department of the Samford University Library.

I wish to express my special appreciation to Ruric Wheeler, Ph.D., Research Professor of Mathematics, Samford University, who reviewed the mathematical procedures used in the study.

Thanks to my former colleague, Fred Hendon, Ph.D., Professor of Economics, Samford University School of Business, for his review of the manuscript and his constructive suggestions.

Contents

Introduction

For the busy reader this study provides an understanding of the way in which free trade contributes to two developments of devastating importance to the United States: (1) the transfer of income producing assets from the United States to foreign ownership at a current annual rate exceeding $500 billion, and (2) the de-industrialization of the United States through movement of manufacturing from the United States to low labor cost countries, particularly China.

This study breaks new ground in that it identifies the destabilization of pricing in the United States domestic market as the cause of the flight of industry from the United States to China, identifies the factors contributing to this destabilization of pricing, and quantifies the contribution of each of these factors, thereby providing a basis for corrective decision making.

Recommended necessary congressional action is presented. It is pointed out that if the Congress does not accept fiscal responsibility and take the needed action: de-industrialization of the United States will continue, the standard of living will decline, the United States will move toward third-world-country status with a sharecropper economy (to borrow Warren Buffet's analogy) enriching foreigners who own the country's income producing assets, and the time will come when the United States will not be able to meet its financial obligations.

However, the Congress finds itself in a trap. The powerful corporate free trade advocates who have built manufacturing plants in China, and who have been substantial contributors to campaign funds of senators and congressmen on both sides of the aisle, can be counted upon to oppose needed legislative reforms.

The Concept of Mercantilism

Mercantilism is a concept of international trade which was at its height during the sixteenth, seventeenth and early eighteenth centuries in Europe. This "mercantile system," as Adam Smith called it, followed the feudal system in European countries. Under mercantilism each country sought to maximize exports, minimize imports and receive payment for the surplus of exports over imports in gold. Because of the universal desirability of precious metals and their worldwide acceptance in exchange, this inflow of gold served the national interest by increasing the wealth of the nation. Governments were active in regulating foreign trade to bring about an excess of exports over imports. In an effort to maintain their export advantage, they prohibited the export of capital equipment and the emigration of skilled labor. They also used tariffs, quotas and other trade barriers to protect their manufacturers from foreign competition. Under mercantilism the total volume of world trade was thought to be fixed. Therefore, the struggle for wealth was a zero-sum endeavor. One nation's gain represented another nation's loss.[1]

Although not as dominant as they were in the sixteenth, seventeenth and early eighteenth centuries, mercantilist policies have continued to be very much alive among the nations of the earth. Even today, subject to the constraints of multinational free trade agreements, most trading nations strive to export more than they import. The United States is the outstanding exception.

Under today's mercantilism, sometimes referred to as neo-mercantilism, a nation strives to achieve a trade surplus (excess of exports over imports); but instead of taking payment for the excess of exports over imports in the form of gold, it takes payment for this difference in income producing assets of its trading partners that have trade deficits (excess of imports over exports). The wealth of a nation with a trade surplus is thereby increased by the amount of its trade surplus and the wealth of a trading partner is decreased by the amount of its trade deficit.

From the United States perspective, here is how it works. Exporters in other countries selling goods to buyers in the United States receive payment for their exported goods in United States dollars. These dollars make their way to the central banks of these exporting countries. Some of these dollars go back to the United States to pay for imports from the United States. The foreign central banks then have on hand the dollars received for the excess of exports to the United States over imports from the United States. These dollars sitting in the central banks are unproductive. To make these dollars earn income they are invested in such United States assets as bonds of the United States government and its agencies, corporate bonds, stocks, real estate investment trust certificates, unincorporated businesses and real estate.

The Concept of Free Trade

Free trade is international trade conducted without governmental interference or regulation. Although free trade in its pure form did not exist, economists in England developed trade models under assumed conditions of free trade.

In 1776 Adam Smith's famous book, *The Wealth of Nations*, was published. In it he proposed an international trading model under which trade between two nations would be beneficial to both nations rather than a zero-sum endeavor. Adam Smith assumed that in a free trade environment each nation would specialize in producing products which it could produce most economically. Nation A would sell to Nation B goods on which it had an absolute cost advantage, taking in payment goods on which Nation B had an absolute cost advantage. A balance of trade was assumed, with neither nation endeavoring to export more than it imported.

In 1817 David Ricardo's *Principles of Political Economy and Taxation* was published. In it Ricardo built on Adam Smith's work by introducing the concept of comparative advantage. Under this concept a nation would export a product on which it had a comparative cost advantage—not necessarily an absolute cost advantage—and would import in exchange a product on which its trading partner had a comparative cost advantage. For example, Country A might be willing to buy product X from Country B even though Country A could produce product X at a cost lower than that of Country B. This could happen if Country A chose to forego producing product X and chose instead to concentrate on producing product Y, on which it had a greater cost advantage. Country A might therefore sell product Y to Country B in exchange for importing product X from Country B.[2]

Reflecting the influence of Adam Smith, England gradually moved in the direction of freer trade. By 1860 England had largely done away with industrial regulations, monopolies and tariffs, and had begun to allow the exportation of machinery and the emigration of skilled labor.[3] The concept of absolute advantage offered by Adam Smith and the concept of comparative advantage offered by David Ricardo have been faithfully reproduced down through the years in economics text books in support of the claim that under free trade everybody benefits. It is no wonder that students come out of Economics 101 firmly convinced that free trade is beneficial to everyone and is therefore something to be fostered. This way of thinking is so prevalent that favoring free trade has become the politically correct position for politicians regardless of party affiliation. The free trade believers appear oblivious to the fact that the simplistic economic models used by Smith and Ricardo did not then, and do not now, describe the real world. The blind faith of free trade believers has tended to make free trade a political sacred cow in the United States.

Multinational Free Trade Agreements

Following World War II, in 1947 the leading trading nations of the world established the General Agreement on Tariffs and Trade, commonly referred to as GATT. Today more than one hundred nations, accounting for 80 percent of world trade, are GATT participants. From time to time over the years prior to 1986, representatives of participating nations met to negotiate changes in tariffs and related trade matters.

At the meeting in 1986, known as the Uruguay Round of GATT, drastic changes were proposed by multinational corporations, working through the United States representatives. In addition to the objective of establishing a worldwide free trade area by removing all barriers to trade among nations, they demanded the following: (1) that companies be free to invest anywhere in the world without restrictions, (2) that environmental and safety standards throughout the world be "harmonized" or made the same everywhere, which means that the higher standards would be brought down to conform to the lower ones, (3) that the intellectual property rights of patents and trademarks be enforced throughout the world, and (4) that food, agricultural products and such services as banking, insurance and shipping be brought under GATT's control. They also proposed adoption of an administrative structure called the Multilateral Trade Organization, designed to increase GATT's power over all of the participating countries, and to limit their freedom to place restrictions on businesses engaged in international trade. GATT, as revised, now functions under the name of the World Trade Organization (WTO).

A majority of the WTO members are third world countries. These countries are opposed to including labor rights or environmental protection provisions in trade agreements. They consider lax pollution controls and low wages as important assets which they can offer prospective investors.[4]

In 1990 George Bush announced his proposal for the North American Free Trade Agreement (NAFTA), an organization similar to GATT but applying only to the United States, Canada and Mexico. This agreement was subsequently executed and approved by all parties.

The effect of corporate lobbying and political contributions (including contributions of individuals and political action committees influenced by corporate executives) can be seen in the way Congress used the "fast track" procedure to limit its role in the negotiation and approval of the multinational free trade agreements. Under the fast track procedure Congress was required to approve or disapprove a negotiated trade agreement within 60 to 90 days of the President's submission of the agreement. Both the House and Senate were required to limit debate to not more than 20 hours, and no amendments were allowed. Furthermore, Congress was required to agree to the fast track procedure before the President even began to negotiate. The fear was that without the fast track procedure the general public would become fully aware of the provisions of the trade agreement and would successfully pressure their congressional representatives to reject it.

Corporate representatives were present to advise negotiating teams during negotiations, but representatives of citizens groups and the general public were excluded.

Under the provisions of GATT, if a company moves its manufacturing from the United States to some low labor cost country, the United States cannot legally restrict the importation and sale of that company's goods in the United States domestic market. Any effort to prohibit such importation and sale is considered a "non-tariff trade barrier," which GATT's provisions prohibit.

Under the rules of GATT any party accused of a violation of GATT's provisions is considered guilty until proven innocent. The expense and effort of proving innocence rests with the accused party. The decision of guilt or innocence is made by a panel of GATT bureaucrats who meet in secret and are not accountable to anyone.[5]

Effects of Free Trade on the Trade Balance of the United States

In the free trade environment created by the international free trade agreements three important factors have had a detrimental effect on the trade balance of the United States:

1. The trading nations of the whole world have concentrated on exporting to the United States because of the tremendous size of the United States market. At the same time they have deliberately bought as little as possible from the United States.
2. Large United States retailers, wholesalers and manufacturers have increased their purchases of goods from low labor cost countries and have decreased their purchases of goods made in the United States.
3. Large multinational companies based in the United States have opened plants in low labor cost countries and closed plants in the United States, a move which has transferred to other countries the advanced technologies which they had developed in the United States and increased unemployment in the United States.

The *Statistical Abstracts of the United States: 2003* showed merchandise trade balance data for the United States and 60 of its trading partners for the year 2002.[6]

Data were not available for 23 of those countries including: Algeria, Argentina, Bangladesh, Burma, Cameroon, Chile, Ghana, India, Kuwait, Malaysia, Nepal, Nigeria, Pakistan, Peru, Philippines, Poland, Singapore, Sri Lanka, Sweden, Switzerland, Syria, Trinidad and Tobago, and Venezuela.

Of the countries for which data were available, 15 had negative merchandise trade balances (deficits); 22 had positive merchandise trade balances (surpluses). Listed here in declining order are the countries which had negative merchandise trade balances:

	(Millions)
United States	- $497,380
United Kingdom	- 53,050
Spain	- 33,098
Greece	- 21,452
Portugal	- 12,411
Turkey	- 8,635
Mexico	- 7,995
Egypt	- 5,747
Australia	- 5,428
Israel	- 3,757
Morocco	- 3,036
Romania	- 2,613
Hungary	- 2,119
Ecuador	- 1,004
Sudan	- 204

Listed here in declining order are the countries with positive merchandise trade balances:

	(Millions)
Germany	$122,180
Japan	93,830
China	44,167
Saudi Arabia	42,037
Canada	36,838
Ireland	34,898
Netherlands	25,754
Norway	24,371
Indonesia	23,212
Italy	16,533
South Korea	14,180
Finland	13,146
Brazil	13,143
Thailand	9,775
France	8,990
Denmark	8,360
Belgium	8,118
South Africa	4,372
Austria	3,572
Cote d'Ivoire	2,745
Congo	1,598
Columbia	228

The shocking figure in the data provided above is the huge merchandise trade deficit of the United States, $497,380 million, almost $500 billion. The United States appears to be the only trading country in the world that makes no serious effort to achieve a balance, if not a surplus, in its foreign trade.

In 2003 imports represented 36.1% of merchandise used in the United States.[7]

Unemployment in the United States

As a result of layoffs and plant closings, unemployment of manufacturing workers in the United States has soared. As a percentage of all nonagricultural United States employees, manufacturing employees dropped from 28.4% in 1960 to 11% in 2003—a decline of 61%.[8] Three million manufacturing jobs have been lost in the United States over a period of three years.[9] Between July, 2000 and October, 2003 the country lost 2,729,000 manufacturing jobs, amounting to 16 percent of all manufacturing jobs.[10] These laid-off employees were among the highest paid workers in the country. The wages of manufacturing workers are about 20 percent higher than for all other workers in the United States.[11] Laid-off manufacturing workers who have found other employment have generally had to accept lower wages.

It is reported that two-thirds of the people who lose their jobs in the United States do not find employment by the end of the 39-week period during which they draw unemployment benefits. Because the government does not keep track of unemployed individuals after their unemployment benefits run out, the accuracy of unemployment estimates is questionable.[12]

In addition to creating unemployment, the movement of manufacturing from the United States robs the country of technological advantages gained by years of research and manufacturing experience. The availability of specialized skills and know-how is lost when laid-off management personnel and workers switch to other types of employment. Also, with the transfer of industry from the country the United States loses domestic sources of goods that might be critical in time of war.

Stability of Labor Costs in Countries with High Labor Surpluses

In the western world increased productivity has generally led to increased wages. However, in third world countries with high amounts of surplus labor, productivity increases are not likely to be accompanied by significant increases in wages. In such countries instances have been cited in which productivity increases have actually been accompanied by decreases in wages. Stephen Golub, an economist at Swarthmore College cited an instance in Mexico in which productivity increased by 36 percent and wages fell by 19 percent. The stability of low wages in high labor surplus countries makes these countries even more attractive as plant location sites for United States and other multinational companies.[13]

United States Manufacturing and Financial Sector Changes

As manufacturing in the United States has declined, reflecting increased movement of United States manufacturing to other countries and increased reliance of the United States on imports, the financial sector has expanded its services to other countries. According to Bridgewater Associates, as reported in U.S. News and World Report, the financial sector now accounts for 44 percent of United States corporate profits. Since the 1960's the profit share of the manufacturing sector has declined from 50 percent to 10 percent of United States corporate profits.[14] This decrease in profitability of manufacturing in the United States reflects the effect of price competition with cheap imports and the exodus of manufacturing facilities.

Alan Tonelson points out in his book, *Race to the Bottom*, that developing countries have an "anti-consumption bias." They discourage importation of consumer goods. Their imports from the United States are predominantly producer goods, such as machinery and equipment for manufacturing plants.[15]

For several eastern developing countries the 2003 imports from the United States and the percentages of these in manufacturing and transportation equipment are as follows:[16]

Exhibit 1
2003 IMPORTS FROM THE US BY COUNTRY
WITH % IN MACHINERY AND
TRANSPORTATION EQUIPMENT

Country	2003 Imports from the US (Millions of $)	Percent Machinery & Transportation Equipment
China	28,418	44.1
India	4,986	40.4
Indonesia	2,520	26.3
Malaysia	10,921	79.7
Philippines	7,992	78.7
Taiwan	17,488	52.9
Thailand	5,842	55.5

By importing producer goods the developing countries are expanding their capacity to produce consumer goods for export and domestic consumption. At the same time they are developing their capacity to make their own producer goods. These developments may be expected to have a depressing effect on United States exports in the existing free market environment.

Influence of Education

Some low labor cost countries appear to have surpassed the United States in educating their young people for high tech employment. The combination of low wages and education for high tech employment has proven attractive to United States businesses. For example, more than 200 Fortune 500 companies have outsourced work to India.[17] Infosys (Nasdaq: INFY) is an Indian company that specializes in negotiating such outsourcing agreements with United States companies.

The outsourcing of high tech work to low labor cost countries has a discouraging effect on high tech employees in the United States and on the aspirations of young people considering high tech careers.

China Favored for Outsourcing and Plant Investment

In recent years the outsourcing of United States companies has tended to go largely to China. Wal-Mart, Target, J.C. Penny and Federated Department Stores are among the United States retailers buying large quantities of goods from China. Wal-Mart's purchases alone are reported to be $12 billion per year.[18]

In the movement of manufacturing facilities from the United States to low labor cost countries the United States companies have also tended to favor China. United States companies have invested $45 billion in China.[19] More than 450 United States manufacturers now have plants in China. They employ more than 250,000 Chinese workers, and have combined annual sales of $23 billion. Long established brand names such as Motorola, Black and Decker and Levi's are now among the many products sold in the United States but made in China. China is now the source of 80 percent of the toys, 90 percent of the sporting goods and 95 percent of the shoes sold in the United States.[20]

General Motors has invested more than $2 billion in Chinese joint ventures which now make and sell Chevrolets and Buicks as well as domestic brands. With the addition of Cadillacs, they expect these sales to reach 300,000 vehicles per year by the end of 2005.[21]

United States China Business Council (USCBC)

United States companies with interests in China have their own public relations and lobbying organization, the United States China Business Council.[22] Founded in 1973, this organization has more than 300 corporate members. It maintains offices in Washington, D.C., Beijing, Shanghai, and Hong Kong.[23]

The United States China Business Council (USCBC) is a formidable and well-staffed organization. It provides a wide range of advisory and market research services to its member companies. Its publicity and lobbying activities include: (1) Advocating the interests of its member companies before the governments of the United States and China through individual meetings with government officials, (2) providing the media on a continuing basis with information favorable to the interests of USCBC member companies, (3) providing regular briefings for members of Congress and their staffs to discuss United States commercial interests in China in a light favorable to their member companies, and (4) communicating regularly with United States government agencies involved in United States-China trade to gain favorable treatment for their member companies. In addition the USCBC publishes a magazine called *The China*

Business Review and a weekly news letter called *China Market Intelligence.*[24]

In testifying before the Subcommittee on East Asia and Pacific Affairs Senate Foreign Relations Committee, Robert A. Kapp, President of the United States China Business Council, acknowledged the Council's extraordinary lobbying activity with the following statement: "The Council has long enjoyed productive and close engagement with many Members of the Senate and House, many Committees and Subcommittees, and many members of Congressional Staff. We welcome such contacts, and believe that the Council can provide dispassionate and accurate information and perspectives to our counterparts on Capital Hill, as we do to many in the executive branch and to our business constituents."[25]

Growth in the United States Trade Deficit with China

The last year in which the United States had a favorable trade balance was 1975. Under free trade the United States trade deficit has ballooned from $19.4 billion in 1980 to $617.1 billion in 2004.[26] China is the largest contributor to the United States trade deficit. The United States trade deficit with China alone reached $161.9 billion in 2004. In 2004 United States imports from China amounted to $169.7 billion. United States exports to China were $34.7 billion.[27] It is expected that the United States trade deficit with China will reach $300 billion within three years if present trends continue.[28]

Exhibit 2 reflects the escalating recent growth of United States imports from China. It is noted that the imports from China in 2004 exceeded those of 2003 by approximately 30 percent. The only decrease was in Petroleum & Coal Products. The greatest dollar volume increase was for Computer and Electronic Products, which increased almost 47 percent to a total of $63.9 billion for 2004.[29]

EXHIBIT 2
DOLLAR VALUE OF US IMPORTS FROM CHINA FOR
YEARS 2003 AND 2004 AND PERCENT INCREASE FROM
2003 TO 2004 FOR SELECTED INDUSTRY GROUPS

NAICS Code	Industry Groups	2003 Value of Imports ($1,000's)	2004 Value of Imports ($1,000's)	Percent Increase
311	Food and Kindred Products	1,011,530	1,280,416	26.58
312	Beverages & Tobacco Prod.	26,001	31,911	22.73
313	Textiles and Fabrics	529,374	666,382	25.88
314	Textile Mill Products	3,335,035	4,412,749	32.31
315	Apparel & Accessories	11,000,499	13,106,398	19.14
316	Leather & Allied Products	13,787,930	15,442,048	12.00
321	Wood Products	1,284,096	1,821,816	41.88
322	Paper	1,153,280	1,360,325	17.95
323	Printed Matter & Related Prod.	1,121,294	1,414,408	26.14
324	Petroleum & Coal Products	287,478	228,053	(20.67)
325	Chemicals	2,623,975	3,380,551	28.83
326	Plastics & Rubber Products	3,966,302	5,028,421	26.78
327	Nonmetallic Mineral Products	3,013,791	3,419,077	13.45
331	Primary Metal Mfg.	973,665	3,049,775	213.23
332	Fabricated Metal Prod, Nesoi	5,805,443	7,549,630	30.04
333	Machinery, Except Electrical	8,314,396	11,169,237	34.34
334	Computer & Electronic Prod.	43,615,657	63,905,745	46.52
335	Elec. Eq. Appliances, Compnts.	11,814,878	14,735,357	24.72
336	Transportation Equipment	2,890,697	4,144,778	43.36
337	Furniture & Fixtures	8,504,743	10,440,144	22.76
339	Misc. Mfg. Commodities	22,917,728	25,066,309	9.38
	Totals	147,977,792	191,653,530	29.52

Research in China

China is now training 600,000 engineers per year.[30] Analysts estimate China's technological know-how to be only five to ten years behind that of the United States. Large western companies are investing more in research programs in China. For example, it is reported that Microsoft is planning to invest $750 million in such research programs, Motorola, $1.3 billlion.[31] This outsourcing of research work, along with the outsourcing of computer programming, is causing loss of jobs among highly paid technical people in the United States.

The shifting of research to other countries also means that an increasing amount of the research leading to development of new products and new industries is being done abroad.

China's Manufacturing Growth

In recent years China's trade has grown three times faster than that of the rest of the world.[32] China now makes 50 percent of the world's cameras, 30 percent of its television sets and air conditioners, 25 percent of the washing machines and 20 percent of the refrigerators. In addition China is heavily into the manufacture of machine tools, plastics, semiconductors and computers.[33] Following the United States, Germany and Japan, China is now the world's fourth largest industrial producer.[34]

Dismantled Plant Shipped to China

In some instances manufacturing facilities in the United States are actually dismantled and shipped to China. According to an Associated Press article, that is exactly what is happening to the Gulf States Steel plant in Gadsden, Alabama. This plant previously employed 1,700 people.[35]

Currency Manipulation in Foreign Exchange

Following World War I the gold standard was no longer the basis for the international monetary system. At that time countries discovered that they could use currency manipulation to gain a foreign trade advantage. Devaluation of a country's currency in foreign exchange caused a decrease in prices paid for the country's goods by foreign customers. This stimulated exports, while at the same time it caused an increase in local currency prices of imports, which discouraged imports. However, other countries were free to take counter measures. Many countries experimented with this "competitive devaluation" during the depression of the nineteen thirties. There was a substantial reduction in world trade at that time.[36]

To devalue its currency in foreign exchange Country A could peg the value of its monetary unit to that of a trading partner, Country B, with the value of Country A's currency below what it would be if both countries let their currencies float. A weak country often pegs its currency to that of a stronger trading partner in order to maintain stability for its exchange rate with that country. Pegging does not necessarily imply that one country is devaluing its currency with respect to that of the country to which it is pegged. In 1998, of the 184 IMF (International Monetary Fund) member countries, 48 pegged the value of their currencies to the currencies of other countries.

Eighteen of these pegged the value of their currencies to the United States dollar.[37]

At the present time China is an outstanding example of a country that has used pegging in the devaluation of its currency. China has pegged the undervalued Chinese yuan to the United States dollar.

In mid 2003 a continuing decline in the value of the United States dollar was well underway. The immediate effect of this was to make United States goods cheaper abroad, thereby stimulating United States export sales, and to make United States goods cheaper at home, thereby making United States goods more competitive against imports. The reaction of other countries, notably Japan and other eastern countries, was to devalue their currencies in order to maintain a competitive advantage both in selling to the United States and in minimizing imports from the United States. Foreign trade is still regarded primarily as a zero sum endeavor.

The great sensitivity of other trading countries to changes in the value of the United States dollar is explained by Steve Roach, Chief Economist for Morgan Stanley. As he puts it, "The United States has become the world's buyer of last resort, the place where everyone else sells to, and this has resulted in a global over dependence on the United States economy."[38] This global over dependence on selling to the United States is a consequence of the international free trade agreements negotiated by the United States at the behest of the corporate free trade advocates.

Reasons for China's Foreign Trade Cost Advantage

With respect to selling in the United States domestic market, China's cost advantage over the United States is derived from three sources: (1) China's lower cost of labor, (2) China's pegging of the undervalued Chinese yuan to the United States dollar, and (3) export pricing by Chinese firms based on variable costs only, after overhead has been fully recovered from sales in China.

Cost Advantage of Using Low Cost Chinese Labor

First let's look at the costs of manufacturing goods in the United States for the 21 three-digit manufacturing industry groups of the North American Industrial Classification System (NAICS). The percentages shown in Exhibit 3 were derived from cost data for these manufacturing industry groups collected in the Annual Survey of Manufacturing Industry Groups for 2001 by the United States Census Bureau. As of early 2005 these were the most recent such costs available from the United States Census Bureau.[39] The dollar data from which the Table 3 percentages were derived are shown in the Mathematical Appendix

Exhibit 3
MANUFACTURING COST AS PERCENT OF TOTAL DOLLAR COST OF GOODS PRODUCED IN THE UNITED STATES FOR SELECTED INDUSTRY GROUPS

Industry Groups NAICS Code	1 Direct Labor	2 Materials	3 Direct Energy	4 Indirect Labor	5 Non-Labor Overhead	6 Total Cost
311	6.31	57.31	0.86	3.34	32.18	100.00
312	2.87	35.09	0.36	3.04	58.64	100.00
313	12.77	57.60	1.88	4.83	22.72	100.00
314	10.63	59.98	0.71	5.17	23.51	100.00
315	10.88	53.58	0.33	5.98	29.23	100.00
316	10.68	52.09	0.50	6.11	30.62	100.00
321	12.76	61.65	0.99	4.93	19.67	100.00
322	9.64	43.15	2.34	4.60	30.27	100.00
323	16.81	39.77	0.63	10.13	32.66	100.00
324	1.67	77.96	1.76	1.05	17.56	100.00
325	4.67	48.16	1.86	5.32	39.99	100.00
326	12.70	48.98	1.18	6.35	30.79	100.00
327	13.23	43.69	2.63	5.89	34.56	100.00
331	11.56	60.26	3.15	4.49	20.54	100.00
332	14.97	44.83	0.88	8.56	30.76	100.00
333	10.28	49.83	0.42	9.54	29.93	100.00
334	6.14	47.19	0.31	11.82	34.54	100.00
335	9.79	50.09	0.50	7.28	32.34	100.00
336	6.42	46.69	0.26	3.60	43.03	100.00
337	15.53	44.65	0.50	7.96	31.36	100.00
339	10.39	38.73	0.41	11.11	39.36	100.00
Averages	10.03	51.02	1.07	6.24	31.63	100.00
Wtd. Avg.	9.42	47.82	0.57	9.01	33.18	100.00

Source: These percentage data are derived from: Statistics for Industry Groups and Industries: 2001, Annual Survey of Manufacturers, Tables 2 and 4, Census Bureau, U.S. Department of Commerce (Most recent data). Weighting for weighted averages is based on dollar value 2004 U.S. imports from China, U.S. Census Bureau, Foreign Trade Statistics.

China's labor cost advantage is easy to see. The average manufacturing wage in China has been estimated at 61 cents per hour, compared to $16 dollars per hour in the United States.[40] China's labor cost per hour is about 3.8% of the United States labor cost. This we round to 4% for our calculations. Thus we see that China's labor cost is 96% lower than that of the United States. This cost advantage applies only to direct labor and indirect labor cost segments which appear in Col. 1 and Col. 4 of Exhibit 3. For the industries shown in Exhibit 3, direct labor cost as a percent of total cost using United States labor varies from 1.67% to 15.53%, with an average of 10.03% of total cost. Indirect labor cost as a percent of total cost using United States labor varies from 1.05% to 11.82%, with an average of 6.24% of total cost.

In Exhibit 4 the costs of labor shown in Col. 1 and Col. 4 have been reduced by 96% to reflect the use of Chinese labor.

Exhibit 4

MANUFACTURING COST AS PERCENT OF TOTAL DOLLAR COST OF GOODS PRODUCED IN THE UNITED STATES FOR SELECTED INDUSTRY GROUPS, LESS 96% LABOR COST REDUCTION DUE TO USE OF CHINESE LABOR

	1	2	3	4	5	6
Industry Groups NAICS Code	Direct Labor	Materials	Direct Energy	Indirect Labor	Non-Labor Overhead	Total Cost
311	0.25	57.31	0.86	0.13	32.18	90.73
312	0.11	35.09	0.36	0.12	58.64	94.32
313	0.51	57.60	1.88	0.19	22.72	83.10
314	0.43	59.98	0.71	0.21	23.51	84.84
315	0.44	53.58	0.33	0.24	29.23	83.82
316	0.43	52.09	0.50	0.24	30.62	83.88
321	0.51	61.65	0.99	0.20	19.67	83.02
322	0.39	43.15	2.34	0.18	30.27	86.33
323	0.67	39.77	0.63	0.41	32.66	74.14
324	0.07	77.96	1.76	0.04	17.56	97.39
325	0.19	48.16	1.86	0.21	39.99	90.41
326	0.51	48.98	1.18	0.25	30.79	81.71
327	0.53	43.69	2.63	0.24	34.56	81.65
331	0.46	60.26	3.15	0.18	20.54	84.59
332	0.60	44.83	0.88	0.34	30.76	77.41
333	0.41	49.83	0.42	0.38	29.93	80.97
334	0.25	47.19	0.31	0.47	34.54	82.76
335	0.39	50.09	0.50	0.29	32.34	83.61
336	0.26	46.69	0.26	0.14	43.03	90.38
337	0.52	44.65	0.50	0.32	31.36	77.35
339	0.42	38.73	0.41	0.44	39.36	79.36
Averages	0.40	51.02	1.07	0.25	31.63	84.37
Wtd. Avg.	0.37	47.82	0.57	0.36	33.18	82.30

Note: Col. 6 figure for each industry group represents total cost of production with labor shown at the cost of Chinese labor, expressed as a percentage of what it would cost if produced in the United States with United States labor.

After allowing a 96 percent reduction in direct and indirect labor costs due to use of Chinese Labor, Col. 6 of Exhibit 4 shows the total manufacturing cost for each industry group expressed as a percentage of total cost of production in the United States. At the bottom of Col. 6 of Exhibit 4 we see both average total cost and weighted average total cost as a percent of total United States manufacturing cost. The average total cost includes some error because the value of United States imports from China is not the same for all of the industry groups. We correct for this error by calculating a weighted average total cost based on actual 2004 United States imports from China for the various industry groups. This weighting procedure is explained in the Mathematical Appendix. The weighted average cost of production using Chinese labor is 82.30% of total United States cost of production. Subtracting 82.30% from 100% gives an indicated cost saving of 17.70% due to the use of Chinese labor.

Added Cost Advantage of China's Pegging of the Undervalued Yuan to the United States Dollar

Since 1994 China has pegged its currency in the range of from 8.276 to 8.280 yuan to the United States dollar.[41] This is a relationship which the United States National Association of Manufacturers (NAM) says undervalues the yuan by as much as 40 percent.[42] The NAM further states that reports from investment banks and the Manufacturers' Alliance provided estimates of China's undervaluation of its currency ranging from 15 to 50 percent.[43] Economists have estimated that if China were to let its currency float in foreign exchange, one United States dollar would be equal to about 5 yuan.[44] This corresponds with an undervaluation of the yuan of approximately 40 percent, which is probably about right.

This pegging of the undervalued Chinese yuan to the United States dollar is assumed to give the producer in China an added cost advantage of forty percent on all costs of manufacturing other than direct labor and indirect labor. This cost advantage applies to the costs of materials, direct energy and non-labor overhead.

Exhibit 5 reflects for each industry group a 96 percent reduction in direct and indirect labor cost and a 40 percent reduction in the costs of materials, direct energy and non-labor overhead.

Exhibit 5
MANUFACTURING COSTS AS PERCENT OF TOTAL
DOLLAR COST OF GOODS PRODUCED IN THE US FOR
SELECTED INDUSTRY GROUPS, LESS 96% OF LABOR
COSTS DUE TO USE OF CHINESE LABOR AND 40%
REDUCTION IN OTHER COSTS DUE TO PEGGING OF THE
UNDERVALUED YUAN TO THE US DOLLAR

	1	2	3	4	5	6
Industry Groups NAICS Code	Direct Labor	Materials	Direct Energy	Indirect Labor	Non-Labor Overhead	Total Cost
311	0.25	34.39	0.52	0.13	19.31	54.60
312	0.11	21.05	0.22	0.12	35.18	56.68
313	0.51	34.68	1.13	0.19	13.63	50.14
314	0.43	35.99	0.43	0.21	14.11	51.17
315	0.44	32.15	0.20	0.24	17.54	18.42
316	0.43	31.25	0.30	0.24	18.37	50.59
321	0.51	36.99	0.59	0.20	11.80	50.09
322	0.39	31.89	1.40	0.18	18.16	52.02
323	0.67	23.86	0.38	0.41	19.60	44.92
324	0.07	46.78	1.05	0.04	10.54	58.49
325	0.19	28.90	1.12	0.21	23.99	54.41
326	0.51	29.39	0.71	0.25	18.47	49.33
327	0.53	26.21	1.58	0.24	20.74	49.30
331	0.46	36.16	1.89	0.18	12.32	51.01
332	0.60	26.90	0.53	0.34	18.46	46.83
333	0.41	29.90	0.25	0.38	17.96	48.90
334	0.25	28.31	0.19	0.47	20.72	49.94
335	0.39	30.05	0.30	0.29	19.40	50.43
336	0.26	28.01	0.16	0.14	25.82	54.39
337	0.52	26.79	0.30	0.32	18.82	46.75
339	0.42	23.24	0.25	0.44	23.62	47.97
Averages	0.40	29.08	0.64	0.25	18.98	49.35
Wtd. Avg.	0.37	26.49	0.35	0.36	19.91	47.48

Note: Col. 6 figure for each industry group represents total cost of production in China, expressed as a percent of what it would cost if produced in the United States.

After allowing for a 96 percent reduction in direct and indirect labor costs due to use of Chinese labor and a 40 percent reduction in materials, direct energy and non-labor overhead costs, due to China's pegging of the undervalued Chinese yuan to the United States dollar, the figures shown in Col. 6 of Exhibit 5 represent the total manufacturing costs in China expressed as percentages of total costs if produced in the United States. The weighted average cost of manufacturing in China is only 47.48% of United States total cost (indicating a saving of 52.52%). By subtracting the 17.70% saving due to use of Chinese labor from 52.52% we find the cost saving of 34.82% due to China's pegging of the undervalued Chinese yuan to the United States dollar. Thus we see that the pegging of the undervalued Chinese yuan to the United States dollar is about two times as effective in lowering Chinese manufacturing costs as is the low cost of Chinese labor.

Added Chinese Cost Advantage Based on Consideration of Variable Costs Only— After Overhead Has Been Fully Recovered from Sales in China

Manufacturing costs may be classified as either variable or fixed. Variable costs are those that vary with changes in the volume of production. Fixed costs do not vary with changes in the volume of production. In our example, direct labor, materials and direct energy are variable costs. The overhead costs of indirect labor and non-labor overhead are fixed costs.

For any operating period, once the manufacturer's allocations of revenue toward payment of overhead costs reach the total cost of overhead (indirect labor plus non-labor overhead in our example), overhead costs cease with respect to additional production and only variable costs need to be considered as a floor in pricing the product. If a manufacturer in China is able to recover all of its overhead from sales in China, it can price export sales based on variable costs only.

Exhibit 6
MFG. COSTS AS % OF TOTAL COST OF GOODS
PRODUCED IN THE US FOR SELECTED INDUSTRY
GROUPS, LESS 96% LABOR SAVING FROM USE OF
CHINESE LABOR, 40% REDUCTION IN OTHER COSTS DUE
TO PEGGING THE UNDERVALUED YUAN TO THE US
DOLLAR, AND ELIMINATION OF OVERHEAD AFTER ITS
FULL RECOVERY IN CHINA

Industry Groups NAICS Code	1 Direct Labor	2 Materials	3 Direct Energy	4 Indirect Labor	5 Non-Labor Overhead	6 Total Cost
311	0.25	34.39	0.52	0.00	0.00	35.16
312	0.11	21.05	0.22	0.00	0.00	21.38
313	0.51	34.68	1.13	0.00	0.00	36.32
314	0.43	35.99	0.43	0.00	0.00	36.85
315	0.44	32.15	0.20	0.00	0.00	32.79
316	0.43	31.25	0.30	0.00	0.00	31.96
321	0.51	36.99	0.59	0.00	0.00	38.09
322	0.39	31.89	1.40	0.00	0.00	33.68
323	0.67	23.86	0.38	0.00	0.00	24.91
324	0.07	46.78	1.05	0.00	0.00	47.91
325	0.19	28.90	1.12	0.00	0.00	30.21
326	0.51	29.39	0.71	0.00	0.00	30.61
327	0.53	26.21	1.58	0.00	0.00	28.32
331	0.46	36.16	1.89	0.00	0.00	38.51
332	0.60	26.90	0.53	0.00	0.00	28.03
333	0.41	29.90	0.25	0.00	0.00	30.56
334	0.25	28.31	0.19	0.00	0.00	28.75
335	0.39	30.05	0.30	0.00	0.00	30.74
336	0.26	28.01	0.16	0.00	0.00	28.43
337	0.52	26.79	0.30	0.00	0.00	27.61
339	0.42	23.24	0.25	0.00	0.00	23.91
Averages	0.40	29.08	0.64	0.00	0.00	30.12
Wtd. Avg.	0.37	26.49	0.35	0.00	0.00	27.21

Note: Col. 6 figure for each industry group represents total cost of production in China, expressed as a percent of what it would cost if produced in the United States.

For the selected industry groups, Col. 6 of Exhibit 6 shows costs as a percentage of United States manufacturing costs after allowing for lower Chinese labor costs, effect of China's pegging of the undervalued Chinese yuan to the United States dollar, and elimination of overhead costs after recovery of overhead costs from sales in China.

The Chinese cost advantage could be further increased by government subsidy in the case of any industry in which the Chinese government might seek to attract investment.

By referring to the weighted average total cost in Col. 6 of Exhibit 6, we see that by combining (a) the use of low-cost Chinese labor, (b) China's pegging of the undervalued Chinese yuan to the United States dollar and (c) the recovery of overhead from sales in China, the Chinese producer has a weighted average cost of only 27.21% of United States cost. This is less than one-third of the cost of producing the product in the United States.

Chinese Cost Advantage Assuming 96% Labor Cost Saving from Use of Chinese Labor and Elimination of Overhead Costs after Overhead Has Been Fully Recovered from Sales in China. (It is assumed that China is letting its currency float—no longer pegged to the United States dollar.)

Referring to Exhibit 7 we see that by using Chinese labor, pricing based on variable costs only after recovering overhead from sales in China, and NOT using the pegging of the undervalued Chinese yuan to the United States dollar, the weighted average total cost of manufacturing in China is only 48.76% of United States costs (indicating a cost saving of 51.24%). These low Chinese manufacturing cost figures can be achieved by well-established Chinese producers without the benefit of pegging the undervalued Chinese yuan to the United States dollar.

Exhibit 7

MFG. COST AS % OF TOTAL COST OF GOODS PRODUCED
IN THE US FOR SELECTED INDUSTRY GROUPS, LESS 96%
LABOR SAVINGS FROM USE OF CHINESE LABOR, AND
ELIMINATION OF OVERHEAD COSTS AFTER OVERHEAD
HAS BEEN RECOVERED FROM SALES IN CHINA. IT IS
ASSUMED THAT CHINA IS LETTING ITS CURRENCY
FLOAT (NOT PEGGED TO THE UNITED STATES DOLLAR)

Industry Groups NAICS Code	1 Direct Labor	2 Materials	3 Direct Energy	4 Indirect Labor	5 Non-Labor Overhead	6 Total Cost
311	0.25	57.31	0.86	0.00	0.00	58.42
312	0.11	35.09	0.36	0.00	0.00	35.56
313	0.51	57.60	1.88	0.00	0.00	60.19
314	0.43	59.98	0.71	0.00	0.00	61.12
315	0.44	53.58	0.33	0.00	0.00	54.35
316	0.43	52.09	0.50	0.00	0.00	53.02
321	0.51	61.65	0.99	0.00	0.00	63.15
322	0.39	43.15	2.34	0.00	0.00	55.88
323	0.67	39.77	0.63	0.00	0.00	41.07
324	0.07	77.96	1.76	0.00	0.00	79.79
325	0.19	48.16	1.86	0.00	0.00	50.21
326	0.51	48.98	1.18	0.00	0.00	50.67
327	0.53	43.69	2.63	0.00	0.00	46.85
331	0.46	60.26	3.15	0.00	0.00	63.87
332	0.60	44.83	0.88	0.00	0.00	46.31
333	0.41	49.83	0.42	0.00	0.00	50.66
334	0.25	47.19	0.31	0.00	0.00	47.75
335	0.39	50.09	0.50	0.00	0.00	50.98
336	0.26	46.69	0.26	0.00	0.00	47.21
337	0.52	44.65	0.50	0.00	0.00	45.67
339	0.42	38.73	0.41	0.00	0.00	39.56
Averages	0.40	51.02	1.07	0.00	0.00	52.49
Wtd. Avg.	0.37	47.82	0.57	0.00	0.00	48.76

Note: Col. 6 figure for each industry group represents total cost of the product produced in China, expressed as a percent of what it would cost if produced in the United States.

Destabilization of Pricing in the United States Domestic Market

The individual Chinese cost advantages are:
a. Low Labor Costs
b. Pegging of the Undervalued Chinese Yuan to the United States Dollar
c. Pricing Based on Variable Costs Only after Overhead Has Been Fully Recovered from Sales in China.

Exhibit 8
WEIGHTED AVERAGE TOTAL CHINESE COSTS AS % OF US COSTS AND CORRESPONDING COST SAVINGS AS % OF US COSTS, USING SPECIFIC CHINESE COST ADVANTAGES AS SET OUT IN EXHIBITS 4 THROUGH 7

Exhibits	Chinese Cost Advantages	Weighted Average Total Chinese Costs As % of US Costs	Cost Savings As % of US Costs
4	a	82.30	17.70
5	a, b	47.48	52.52
6	a, b, c	27.21	72.79
7	a, c	48.76	51.24

In Exhibit 8 we see that the manufacturing cost savings from use of low cost Chinese labor is 17.70%. While this is a significant saving and could well be sufficient to cause some companies from other countries to build plants in China or buy from Chinese sources, this is not the incentive that caused the wholesale movement of manufacturing from the United States and other countries to China.

In Exhibit 8 we see that when China's low cost of labor is combined with the pegging of the undervalued Chinese yuan to the United States dollar, the costs of the Chinese manufacturer amount to only 47.48% of what it would cost to produce the product in the United States. This is a cost saving of 52.52% of United States costs. Low cost labor accounts for only 17.70% of this. Pegging of the undervalued Chinese yuan to the United States dollar accounts for the difference of 34.82%. Thus we see that the pegging of the undervalued Chinese yuan to the United States dollar has about two times the cost lowering effect as the use of low cost Chinese labor.

With a cost advantage of greater than 50%, the producer in China is able to sell in the United States at prices that destabilize pricing in the United States domestic market.

What do we mean by destabilization of pricing in the United States domestic market? We mean that the producer in China is able to sell profitably in the United States at prices so low that its competitor in the United States must either go out of business, buy its products from a Chinese source, or move its manufacturing to China.

Pegging of the undervalued Chinese yuan to the United States dollar provides THE distinctive Chinese cost advantage. It is the primary reason why United States companies have moved manufacturing to China.

It is also the primary reason why manufacturers in other countries have set up shop in China.

Because of the pegging of the undervalued Chinese yuan to the United States dollar, a manufacturer moving to China from the United States or any other country, including both high labor cost countries and low labor cost countries, gains a substantial cost advantage in selling to the United States and to other countries.

Referring again to Exhibit 8 we see that once a manufacturer producing in China becomes well enough established to recover all of its overhead costs from sales in China, it is able to achieve total manufacturing cost of only 27.21% of the United States cost of producing the product—a saving of 72.79%.

In Exhibit 8 we see that making use of low cost Chinese labor and of pricing based on variable costs only after overhead has been fully recovered from sales in China, weighted average total Chinese costs are only 48.76% of total United States costs—a saving of 51.24%. This combination is still sufficient to cause the destabilization of pricing in the United States domestic market with respect to products sold by these manufacturers.

Note that the advantages, low labor costs and pricing based on variable costs only after overhead costs have been fully recovered, are not exclusively Chinese. In any low labor cost country established manufacturers can achieve similar cost results.

Here are a couple of examples of the problems United States manufacturers face in the United States domestic market where pricing has been destabilized.

American Metal Ware had to close its factory in Wisconsin because a Chinese manufacturer "stole the design of its product" and made copies which it sold at half price in the United States. In order to stay in business American Metal Ware moved its manufacturing to China.[45]

Jay Bender, President of Falcon Plastics, Inc., testified that he had previously sold a particular mold to former customers at a competitive price of $25,000. He lost these customers because they were able to purchase the same mold from a Chinese source for $3,000. That price was less than Falcon's cost of materials and components on the world market. Because of competition from China, Falcon has had to reduce its work force from 300 to 200 people. Mr. Bender reported that one of his customers, a large manufacturer of fishing lures, was able to realize a 50 percent reduction in its manufacturing costs by moving to China.[46]

China's High De Facto Tariff Against Imports from the United States

China's pegging of the undervalued yuan to the United States dollar accomplishes two things: (1) It gives producers in China lower costs, enabling them to sell cheaper in the United States domestic market; and (2) it erects a high de facto tariff barrier against imports to China from the United States. How high is this barrier against imports to China from the United States? To find out, let's take a look at Exhibit 9, International Trade Cost Relationships.

Exhibit 9
INTERNATIONAL TRADE COST RELATIONSHIPS

(1) Low-cost Country's Unit Cost	(2) High-cost Country's Unit Cost	(3) International Unit Cost Difference	(4) High-cost Country's Import Discount	(5) Low-cost Country's Import Premium
$9.00	$10	$1.00	10%	11%
$8.50	$10	$1.50	15%	18%
$8.00	$10	$2.00	20%	25%
$7.50	$10	$2.50	25%	33%
$7.00	$10	$3.00	30%	43%
$6.50	$10	$3.50	35%	54%
$6.00	$10	$4.00	40%	67%
$5.50	$10	$4.50	45%	82%
$5.00	$10	$5.00	50%	100%
$4.50	$10	$5.50	55%	122%
$4.00	$10	$6.00	60%	150%

Column 3 = Column 2 minus Column 1.
Column 4 = Column 3 as a percentage of Column 2.
Column 5 = Column 3 as a percentage of Column 1.

Exhibit 9 involves a product for which the total cost of production in the United States (High Cost Country) is $10 per unit, as shown in Col. 2.

For the same product, Col. 1, Low Cost Country's Unit Cost, shows a range of total costs per unit from $9.00 down to $4.00, which might be appropriate for a country such as China.

Col. 3, International Unit Cost Difference, shows values representing Col. 2 minus Col. 1.

Col. 4, High Cost Country's Import Discount (Col. 3 as a percentage of Col. 2) shows the maximum percentage of total cost which the High Cost Country Purchaser could save by importing the product from the Low Cost Country.

Col. 5, Low Cost Country's Import Premium (Col. 3 as a percentage of Col. 1) shows the percentage premium which a Low Cost Country purchaser would have to pay if it imported the product from the High Cost Country instead of buying it from a manufacturer in its own country.

Now let's see what effect the low labor cost of China has upon the Import Premium which a buyer in China would have to pay to import the product from the United States. In Exhibit 8 we see that for the industries listed the weighted average cost as a percent of United States cost is 82.3% and cost saving of

17.70%. This 17.70% represents the High Cost Country's Import Discount shown in Col. 4 of Exhibit 9. By interpolating we see in Col. 5 of Exhibit 9 that due to the use of Chinese Labor the Chinese purchaser's Import Premium is 21.78%, which we round to 22%.

Now let's see the combined effect of China's low labor cost and China's pegging of the undervalued yuan to the United States dollar upon the import premium a buyer in China would have to pay to import the product from the United States. In Exhibit 8 we see that for the industries listed the weighted average cost as a percent of United States cost is 47.48%. The cost saving as a percent of United States cost is 52.52%, which represents the High Cost Country's Import Discount shown in Col. 4 of Exhibit 9. If we enter Col. 4 of Exhibit 9 with 52.52%, by interpolation we see in Col. 5 of Exhibit 9 that the Chinese purchaser's Import Premium is 109.9%, which we round to 110%.

If we subtract the low labor cost portion of 22% from the total of 110% we see that the effect of China's pegging of the undervalued yuan to the United States dollar caused an 88% import premium. The effect of this is the same as if an 88% tariff had been placed by China on all imports from the United States and China's pegging of the undervalued yuan to the United States dollar had not been used. The 88% import premium can be considered as a de facto tariff on imports to China from the United States.

You will notice that in calculating the Chinese import premiums we have not taken into account the added cost advantage which the Chinese producer obtains after it recovers its overhead costs from sales in China and can sell in the United States based on variable manufacturing costs only.

The extremely high Chinese Import Premiums make it almost impossible for United States manufacturers to sell their goods in the Chinese domestic market. Partly for this reason United States manufacturers conclude that if they want to sell their products in China they must manufacture them in China.

Is China's Pegging of Its Undervalued Yuan to the United States Dollar an Act of Warfare?

The book, *Unrestricted Warfare*, was written by two colonels in the Chinese military service, Qiao Liang and Wang Xiangsui.[47] The unrestricted warfare which these Chinese military officers advocate includes numerous non-military actions, which, with or without military force, could be used by one's country to force another nation to submit to its will.

The authors describe a possible use of unrestricted warfare as follows: "If the attacking side secretly musters large amounts of capital without the enemy nation being aware of this at all and launches a sneak attack against its financial markets, then after causing a financial crisis, buries a computer virus and hacker detachment in the opponent's computer system in advance, while at the same time carrying out a network attack against the enemy so that the civilian electricity network, traffic dispatching network, financial transactions network, telephone communications network, and mass media network are completely paralyzed, this will cause the enemy nation to fall into social panic, street riots, and a political crisis. There is finally the forceful bearing down by the army, and military means are utilized in gradual stages until the enemy is forced to sign a dishonorable peace treaty."[48]

The optimum way to accomplish a limited objective could involve use of a combination of means, which would not necessarily involve military force.

Some specific non-military areas of warfare listed by the authors include: (1) financial warfare, (2) trade warfare, (3) resources warfare, (4) economic aid warfare, (5) regulatory warfare, (6) sanction warfare, (7) media warfare, and (8) ideological warfare[49].

Of particular interest to the United States is the area of trade warfare. It appears that China is using trade warfare to bring about a rapid industrialization of China through de-industrialization of the United States. It is logical that this de-industrialization would also take place to some degree in other industrialized nations that let their currencies float in foreign exchange.

The principal means used by China to bring about the destabilization of pricing in the United States domestic market has been the pegging of the undervalued Chinese yuan to the United States dollar in foreign exchange. China's low labor costs alone could not have done it. The authors no doubt understood this because in their discussion of strategy for dealing with an enemy, they refer to the use of currency revaluation or devaluation as "primary".[50]

The international free trade agreements set the stage on which China has been able to use the pegging of the undervalued yuan to the United States dollar to bring about the destabilization of pricing in the United States domestic market. The United States corporate free trade advocates, whose patronage induced the administration to negotiate international free trade agreements to their liking, were quick to recognize the competitive advantage they could gain by manufacturing in China.

China's destabilization of pricing in the United States domestic market has induced company after company to move manufacturing from the United States to China—not only to survive, but to be on the winning side in exploiting destabilized pricing in the United States domestic market. Thus China's trade warfare against the United States has progressed toward rapid industrialization of China and de-industrialization of the United States.

Active interest of the Chinese army in affairs of the United States is not something new. In 1999 the United States Congress named over 3,000 front companies for the Chinese army operating in the United States.[51]

In the introduction to the book, *Unrestricted Warfare, China's Master Plan to Destroy America,* published by Pan American Publishing Company, Al Santoli points out that a Chinese company, Hutchison Whampoa, Ltd., operates the Panama Canal and controls the ports of Balboa and Cristobal at each end of the canal. Isn't it an interesting coincidence that after the United States gave the Panama Canal to Panama, a Chinese company promptly took over its management. Could it be that China's use of non-military warfare was involved in financing and orchestrating the riots which led to President Carter's insistence on giving the canal to Panama? Management control of the Panama Canal and of the ports at the

Atlantic and Pacific ends of the canal give China significant military and intelligence advantages.

By checking its web site (www.hutchison-whampoa.com) one sees that Hutchison Whampoa, Ltd. manages 39 ports in 19 countries throughout Africa, the Middle East, Asia, Europe and the Americas, including 4 ports in Mexico. It appears reasonable to assume that all of these ports are potential bases for clandestine activities of the Chinese Army, and that at the pleasure of the Chinese Army any of these ports could allow passage, in or out, of terrorist groups and their supplies.

The United States Trade Deficit Consequences

The goods Americans buy from foreigners are paid for in United States dollars. Some of these dollars are used to buy goods which foreigners import from the United States. The rest of the dollars paid to foreigners is an amount equal to the United States trade deficit for the year. The current projected total trade deficit for the United States is about $500 billion. The question is, what will the foreigners do with that $500 billion? They will not spend it on United States goods and services. The answer is, they will retain some of it to increase their dollar reserves, but will spend most of it to buy income-producing assets in the United States.

In the year 2002 foreigners owned $1.21 trillion in United States Treasury securities, $1.69 trillion in United States corporate and other bonds, plus $1.17 trillion in United States stocks. A grand total of $4.07 trillion. The total net purchases of United States securities by foreigners in 2002 amounted to $548.9 billion. This total is broken down as follows: (1) United States Treasury bonds and notes $121.7 billion, (2) United States government corporation or agency bonds $195.5 billion, (3) corporate bonds $182.3 billion, and (4) corporate stocks $49.4 billion. The total foreign purchases of debt securities of the United States government and its agencies in 2002 amounted to $317.2 billion. These purchases by foreigners provide the United States government with a source of easy money with which to live beyond its means.[52]

In 2003 foreigners were reported to own 13% of all United States stocks, 24% of all United States corporate bonds and 40% of all United States Treasury bonds and bills.[53]

Warren Buffet has estimated that the United States total national wealth is $50 trillion, and that because of the huge United States trade deficits, ownership of this national wealth is being transferred to foreigners at the rate of one percent per year.[54] If the trade deficits are allowed to continue at the current rate, foreign ownership of United States assets will increase by approximately $1 trillion every two years, and we can look forward to the time when foreigners will be the majority owners of the country's wealth.

In 2003 the income payments to foreigners on assets which they owned in the United States amounted to $252.573 billion. Of this amount payments by the United States government to foreigners on United States treasury securities amounted to $72.042 billion.[55]

The Bank for International Settlements estimated that at the end of 2000 the total world currency reserves amounted to $1.909 trillion. United States dollars comprised 76% of this total or $1.450 trillion.[56] In March of 2004 China was reported to have more than $310 billion in United States dollar reserves.[57]

Foreign Trade Equation

The foreign trade equation set out below may be used to explain the consequences of the deficit creation effect of free trade with respect to the United States economy.

The left side of the equation is the United States current account balance for the year ($530.668 billion for 2003). This includes: (1) the trade deficit for goods and services for the year, adjusted for income receipts and payments for the year ($463.229 billion in 2003) and (2) net governmental and private non-trade transfers of funds abroad for the year ($67.439 billion in 2003).[58]

The right side of the equation consists of (1) net foreign accumulation of dollar reserves for the year and (2) net foreign acquisition of United States assets during the year.

The United States current account negative balance of $530.668 billion for 2003 went immediately into the dollar reserves of foreigners. The substantial increases in dollar reserves of foreign countries place the central banks of these countries under pressure to make these dollars productive by causing them to be invested in the United States.

Some of these dollar reserves are invested directly by the central banks in United States government securities. Others are made available on favorable terms to banks, and through them to some of their large customers, for investment in the United States.

These investments in the United States can include purchases of United States government bonds, corporate bonds, corporate preferred stocks, corporate common stocks, and real estate investment trust certificates. They may also include acquisition of United States companies by foreign companies (Examples: the proposed acquisition of IBM's personal computer business by the Chinese company, Lenovo[59] and the establishment of foreign-owned businesses in the United States, such as the automobile plants built in the United States by Toyota). Foreign purchases may also include direct purchase of investment properties, farm and timberland and mineral resources.

Foreigners appear to have a preference for investments which pay fixed interest rates or dividends. As these opportunities diminish, however, they may be expected to invest more heavily in common stocks of public companies—to the extent of eventually obtaining majority ownership and management control.

Given sufficient time without corrective action, the United States could eventually wake up to find that foreigners control virtually all of United States industry. The population then might well consider themselves to be economic slaves or sharecroppers laboring for foreign owners, to whom the business profits go.

Where will the allegiance of the congressional free trade coalition be when they discover that the free trade corporate patrons to which they are beholden have come under the control of foreigners?

Jobs in Plants Built in the United States by Foreigners

Job-hungry communities all over the United States are competing vigorously to attract the establishment of foreign owned businesses in their communities. They offer such incentives as free plant sites, low interest rate municipal bond financing and exemption from state and local taxes for extended periods of time. It is reported that Toyota was offered incentives worth about $125 million to build a plant in Kentucky.[60]

These foreign companies also receive financial incentives from their home banks, which are under pressure to lend out the dollar reserves with which they are loaded because of the huge United States trade deficits induced by free trade.

Local politicians regard attracting foreign businesses as a great way to create jobs and build prosperity for their communities. In its recent television advertising Toyota claimed to have created 200,000 jobs in the United States.

While these foreign owned businesses do provide jobs to reduce some of the unemployment caused by flight of industry from the United States, they are still a manifestation of the transfer of ownership of United States wealth to foreigners as a result of the huge United States free trade induced trade deficits.

Businesses established in the United States by foreigners enjoy some competitive advantages because:

(1) They are subsidized with low interest rate financing from bankers in their home countries. (2) They are subsidized by local and state governments who compete for them. (3) The United States government subsidizes them by waiving federal taxes on interest income from municipal bonds. (4) They do not have the financial responsibility of long-established retirement programs, as do some of their competitors. (5) They are in most cases not unionized.

Looming United States Financial Catastrophe

Knowledgeable and responsible leaders have warned that irresponsible fiscal policies of the United States government are propelling the country toward economic disaster. Here are a few examples of such warnings:

On September 17, 2003, in a speech before the National Press Club a dire warning of impending disaster was issued by David M. Walker, Director of the United States General Accounting Office (GAO) and Controller General of the United States. On January 4, 2004, at a joint session of the American Economic Foundation (AEF) and the North American Economic and Finance Association (NAEFA) similar warnings were given by three outstanding authorities: Robert E. Rubin, former Secretary of the Treasury; Peter R. Orszag, Senior Fellow at the Brookings Institution; and Allen Sinai, Chief Global Economist at Decision Economics, Inc. Also, on January 7, 2004 the International Monetary Fund (IMF) placed the United States government on notice that its continued huge deficits were carrying the country toward disastrous consequences.[61]

Warren Buffet has added his warning that the administration and the congressional coalition who support the corporate free trade agenda "are building up a trade deficit that could ultimately take down the U.S. economy."[62]

For the United States government the Congressional Budget Office has issued an estimated $422 billion deficit for 2004 and a $2.3 trillion deficit for the next ten years.

Comptroller General David Walker pointed out that this estimate is extremely conservative because it focuses on public debt already incurred. A major fault is that it does not take into account the social security and Medicare obligations for 77 million baby boomers, who will begin retiring in about four years, when the boomers born in 1946 will be eligible for early retirement at age 62.

For the ten-year period following 2004, other analysts have made estimates of the "fiscal gap" showing in today's dollars what it would take to pay off future obligations. These estimates may be compared to the $2.3 trillion estimate by the Congressional Budget Office.

$40.2 trillion (Government Accountability Office)

$72 trillion (Social Security Board of Trustees)

$47 trillion (International Monetary Fund)

$60 trillion (Brookings Institution)

$44 trillion [Jagadeesh Gokhale (with Federal Reserve Bank of Cleveland) and Kent Smetters (former Treasury Department Deputy Assistant Secretary)]

The Medicare trustees say that their $72 trillion fiscal gap estimate consists of $10 trillion for Social Security and $62 trillion for Medicare.[63]

Basic Cause of Both Trade and Operating Deficits

High trade deficits and operating deficits of the United States government have the same root cause: Senators and congressmen cast their votes based more on "How will this proposal affect my reelection?" than on "Is this proposal good for the country?"

<u>With respect to trade deficits</u>: To retain the financial support of corporate free trade advocates, United States senators and congressmen approved the multinational free trade agreements. This brought about the huge trade deficits, causing: the flight of industry from the United States to low labor cost countries, high United States manufacturing unemployment, and the wholesale transfer of America's income producing assets to foreigners.

<u>With respect to the huge operating deficits</u>: Over the years our senators and congressmen have bought votes by giving expensive benefits to various voting blocks without providing the revenues to pay for them. They have ignored the cardinal rule that NO BENEFIT GIVEN BY CONGRESS IS GOOD FOR THE COUNTRY IF IT IS NOT WORTH THE TAXES TO PAY FOR IT.

Summary

1. Large companies based in the United States wanted a free trade system that would remove all barriers to international trade. Under free trade they would be able to avoid the high United States labor costs by moving their manufacturing to low labor cost countries. They would then be able to ship their goods to the United States and profitably undersell their competitors.

2. Corporate free trade advocates, whose political contributions had been substantial to politicians on both sides of the aisle, induced the Administration to negotiate international free trade agreements to their liking, and induced Congress to approve them under a fast track procedure.

3. Under free trade the trading nations of the world concentrated on exporting to the large United States market, and the United States trade deficit mushroomed. Restrictions of the multinational free trade agreements prevented the United States from limiting imports.

4. China pegged its undervalued yuan to the United States dollar in foreign exchange, thereby: (1) bringing about the destabilization of pricing in the United States domestic market with respect to goods produced in China and (2) erecting a high de facto tariff to discourage Chinese importation of goods from the United States.

5. Destabilization of pricing in the United States caused growing United States importation of goods from China. That, along with the de facto tariff against Chinese imports from the United States, brought about an increasing industrialization of China and de-industrialization of the United States.

6. The high United States trade deficit, resulting from free trade and China's pegging of the undervalued Chinese yuan to the United States dollar, puts huge sums of United States dollars in the hands of foreigners, causing increased foreign ownership of United States income producing assets, including heavy foreign purchasing of United States government and government agency securities. This foreign purchasing of United States government securities provides easy money to help the United States government live beyond its means.

7. Under free trade the United States is now financing the prosperity of the rest of the world (particularly developing nations) by allowing build up of its huge trade deficits.

8. The United States is now financing its own prosperity with borrowed money.

9. Due to the huge United States trade deficits, the wealth of the nation is being transferred to foreign ownership at a rate exceeding a trillion dollars every two years.

10. De-industrialization of the United States, accompanied by the export of jobs, technology and research, along with the rapid transfer of ownership

of United States income producing assets to foreigners, is lowering the United States standard of living and pushing the United States toward status as a third-world country with its wealth predominantly owned by foreigners.

11. The large growing operating deficits and debt service are propelling the country toward economic catastrophe when the United States government will not be able to meet its financial obligations.

Action Needed by the United States

1. The United States should nullify the effect of China's pegging of its undervalued yuan to the United States dollar by placing a tariff of 58% or thereabout on all imports from China. The Chinese cost saving due to pegging the undervalued yuan to the United States dollar is estimated as 34.82% of United States manufacturing cost. This represents 58.03% of cost in Chinese currency, which is undervalued by 40%. This tariff should continue in effect until China in good faith lets its currency float in foreign exchange. Here's why:

   • China's pegging of the undervalued yuan to the United States dollar has been the principal cause of the destabilization of pricing in the United States market with respect to products manufactured in China. It has a cost cutting effect of twice that of China's low cost labor, bringing the cost or manufacturing in China down to less than 50% of United States cost, thereby giving United States companies the incentive for manufacturing in China.

   • China's pegging of the undervalued yuan to the United States dollar has erected a high de facto tariff against imports from the United States. This de facto tariff can be more than 80% of a Chinese purchaser's

cost of buying a product from the United
States.

2. With the objective of eliminating the United States
trade deficits, the United States should withdraw
from participating in multinational free trade
agreements, and should use bilateral trade
agreements only, maintaining the freedom to
employ tariffs, quotas and other trade restraints to
restrict imports to acceptable levels. Here's why:

- The multinational free trade agreements
  establish trading rules that prevent the
  United States from limiting imports
  effectively, thereby allowing United States
  trade deficits to grow without limit. The
  trade deficits are settled by transferring to
  foreign ownership United States income
  producing assets, now amounting to more
  than a trillion dollars every two years.

- Under free trade, even with the elimination
  of China's pegging of the undervalued yuan
  to the United States dollar, well established
  manufacturers in China and other low labor
  cost countries can bring about a
  destabilization of pricing in the United
  States domestic market. By pricing their
  goods based on variable costs only, after
  overhead has been recovered from sales in
  their own countries, they can bring their
  costs down to about 50% of United States
  costs, low enough to destabilize pricing in

the United States with respect to their products.

3. The United States government should limit spending and should maintain an operating surplus to use in the continuing reduction of government debt. Here's why:

- Now running operating deficits exceeding $500 billion per year, the United States government is financially out of control and heavily dependent on foreigners, who buy United States government obligations in partial settlement of United States trade deficits.

- Knowledgeable business leaders, economists and financial experts have given warning after warning that the irresponsible fiscal policies of the United States government are propelling the country toward economic disaster. A financial collapse could come suddenly, as it did in Russia, forcing the United States government to default on its obligations.

In an attempt to prevent any United States tariff against Chinese goods that would effectively nullify China's pegging of its undervalued yuan to the United States dollar, China may be expected to propose a piecemeal correction of the undervaluation of the yuan to take place in small increments over many years. United States companies manufacturing in China may be expected to support this approach since it would allow them to continue exploiting the destabilization of pricing in the United States domestic market. From the United States point of view, the only acceptable solution would be for China to let its currency float.

If China changes from pegging the undervalued yuan to the United States dollar to pegging it to some other currency or a group of currencies, you may be sure that the change will be made only if they anticipate that the change will accomplish for them the same advantage over the United States which they got by pegging the undervalued yuan to the United States dollar.

The Free Trade Trap

There are two main reasons why the Congress and the Administration have taken no effective action to curb the flow of United States industry to China and to reduce the huge United States trade deficit.

(1) They fear the loss of political contributions from large corporations that manufacture in China or buy largely from Chinese sources. Without financial support of these corporate free trade advocates they fear they might not be reelected. They like their cushy jobs. (2) They fear that if foreigners stop their heavy purchasing of United States government securities, the government will collapse through inability to meet its current obligations. Dollars going to foreigners due to the high United States trade deficits have provided a ready market for sale of United States government securities, thereby helping the United States government to live beyond its means. Thus the Congress now finds itself caught in a free trade trap of its own making.

After years of concentrating on "What's good for my reelection" instead of "What's good for the country," can Congress be relied upon to take the necessary corrective action? Over the years members of Congress have been given a lot of misinformation about free trade. However, even with a clear understanding of the problems associated with free trade, as set out in this study, it would be very difficult for them to act against the wishes of the corporate free trade advocates who have been their long-time patrons.

More than 450 United States companies have participated in the flight of industry from the United States to China. Motivated by their bottom line interest in profiting from the destabilization of pricing in the United States, they are inadvertent collaborators with a country that is striving to destroy the United States and to replace it as the world's greatest superpower.

What can motivate Congress to take the needed corrective action? Pressure. Pressure from an informed and irate electorate. Pressure strong enough to unseat them if they refuse to take appropriate action.

The information contained in this study needs to be spread throughout the country. This is a job for the media, for factions and individuals opposed to the exportation of United States industries and jobs. For all those who want to stop the wholesale transfer of United States wealth to foreigners due to huge trade deficits. For all those who want the United States government to live within its means without borrowing from foreigners.

Mathematical Appendix

A major objective of this study is to calculate the cost advantage of each of the three factors which account for China's lower manufacturing cost, compared to the cost of manufacturing in the United States. These are (a) China's lower labor cost, (b) China's pegging of the undervalued Chinese yuan to the United States dollar, and (c) China's pricing based on variable costs only after overhead costs have been recovered from sales in China.

In order to make these calculations we need data on the costs of manufacturing in the United States. Our source of the United States manufacturing cost data is: Statistics for Industry Groups and Industries: 2001 Annual Survey of Manufacturers, Tables 2 and 4, Census Bureau, United States Department of Commerce. As of February, 2005 these were the most recent such data available through the United States Census Bureau. Data are presented for each of the three-digit industry groups. These are identified by both industry group name and by NAICS (North American Industry Classification System) code designation. The industry group names and corresponding NAICS code designations are as follows:

NAICS Code	Industry Group Names
311	Food and Kindred Products
312	Beverages & Tobacco Products
313	Textiles and Fabrics
314	Textile Mill Products
315	Apparel & Accessories
316	Leather and Allied Products
321	Wood Products
322	Paper
323	Printed Matter & Related Products
324	Petroleum & Coal Products
325	Chemicals
326	Plastics & Rubber Products
327	Nonmetallic Mineral Products
331	Primary Metal Manufacturing
332	Fabricated Metal Products
333	Machinery, Except Electrical
334	Computer & Electronic Products
335	Electric Equipment, Appliances, Components
336	Transportation Equipment
337	Furniture & Fixtures
339	Miscellaneous Manufactured Commodities

In most of the exhibits throughout the text and in the Mathematical Appendix the industry groups are identified by NAICS code designation only in order to save space.

Appendix Exhibit A
2001 MANUFACTURING COST DATA FOR SELECTED INDUSTRY GROUPS, FROM U S CENSUS BUREAU: STATISTICS FOR INDUSTRY GROUPS & INDUSTRIES IN THOUSANDS OF DOLLARS

	1	2	3	4	5
Industry Groups NAICS Code	Production Workers Wages Tb. 2, Col. E	Total Cost of Materials Tb.2. Col. G	All Employees Payroll Tb.2, Col. B	Purchased Fuels and Elec. Energy Tb.4, Col. A	Total Value of Shipments Tb.2 Col. H
311	28,485,677	258,670,228	43,586,136	7,754,144	451,385,857
312	3,408,631	41,682,936	7,002,720	854,687	118,785,622
313	5,834,249	26,404,199	8,039,762	1,715,624	45,680,697
314	3,399,394	19,176,446	5,051.306	449,758	31,970,642
315	5,938,605	29,253,443	9,204,556	358,845	54,598,294
316	943,433	4,602,267	1,482,565	88,332	8,834,413
321	11,135,413	53,788,662	15,431,017	1,729,205	87,250,016
322	15,026,027	82,822,970	22,188,323	7,314,163	155,846,001
323	16,947,424	40,076,228	27,157,972	1,288,089	100,792,219
324	3,519,479	170,925,808	5,829,969	7,700,311	219,074,798
325	20,465,946	211,145,758	43,800,327	16,321,777	438,410,200
326	21,683,010	83,616,924	32,538,767	4,011,116	170,716,833
327	12,554,146	41,440,307	18,146,912	4,981,351	94,860,574
331	15,984,531	83,301,309	22,199,270	8,708,280	138,245,446
332	37,880,635	113,469,863	59,569,462	4,448,202	253,113,355
333	27,413,602	132,801,489	52,844,234	2,262,150	266,552,878
334	26,372,081	202,645,132	77,137,249	2,697,156	429,470,841
335	11,164,036	57,137,216	19,465,812	1,153,902	114,067,063
336	51,551,334	374,692,947	80,415,734	4,199,728	802,495,870
337	11,207,663	32,207,122	16,950,041	730,261	72,147,131
339	12,075,172	45,004,389	24,988,556	948,701	116,201,090

Source: Statistics for Industry Groups and Industries: 2001 Annual Survey of Manufacturers, Tables 2 and 4, Census Bureau, U S Dept. of Commerce.

The actual cost data from the 2001 Annual Survey of Manufacturers, which were used in this study appear in Appendix Exhibit A. The data shown in Appendix Exhibit B were derived from the data which appear in Appendix Exhibit A.

Appendix Exhibit B

MANUFACTURING COSTS OF GOODS PRODUCED IN THE
US IN 2001 FOR SELECTED INDUSTRY GROUPS IN
THOUSANDS OF DOLLARS

	1	2	3	4	5	6
Industry Groups NAICS Code	Direct Labor	Materials	Direct Energy	Indirect Labor	Non-Labor Overhead	Total Cost
311	28,485,677	258,670,228	3,877,072	15,100,459	145,252,421	451,385,857
312	3,408,631	41,682,936	427,344	3,614,089	69,652,623	118,785,622
313	5,834,249	26,404,199	857,812	2,205,513	10,378,924	45,680,697
314	3,399,394	19,176,446	224,879	1,651,912	7,518,011	31,970,642
315	5,938,605	29,253,443	179,423	3,265,951	15,960,873	54,598,294
316	943,433	4,602,267	44,166	539,132	2,705,415	8,834,413
321	11,135,413	53,788,662	864,603	4,295,604	17,165,735	87,250,016
322	15,026,027	82,822,970	3,657,082	7,162,296	47,177,627	155,846,001
323	16,947,424	40,076,228	644,045	10,210,548	32,913,975	100,792,219
324	3,519,479	170,925,808	3,850,156	2,310,490	38,468,866	219,074,798
325	20,465,946	211,145,758	8,160,889	23,334,381	175,303,227	438,410,200
326	21,683,010	83,616,942	2,005,558	10,855,757	52,555,584	170,716,833
327	12,554,146	41,440,307	2,490,676	5,592,766	32,782,680	94,860,574
331	15,984,531	83,301,309	4,354,140	6,214,739	28,390,727	138,245,446
332	37,880,635	113,469,863	2,224,101	21,688,827	77,849,929	253,113,355
333	27,413,602	132,801,489	1,131,075	25,430,632	79,776,080	266,552,878
334	26,372,081	202,645,132	1,348,578	50,765,168	148,339,882	429,470,841
335	11,164,038	57,137,216	576,951	8,301,774	36,887,057	114,067,036
336	51,551,334	374,692,947	2,050,364	28,864,400	345,336,825	802,495,870
337	11,207,663	32,207,122	395,131	5,742,378	22,624,838	72,147,131
339	12,075,172	45,004,389	474,351	12,913,384	45,733,795	116,201,090

Data from Appendix Exhibit A are rearranged into more useful categories in Appendix Exhibit B.

Direct Labor entries are from Table 2, Col. E, "Production Workers Wages".

Materials entries are from Table 2, Col. G, "Total Cost of Materials".

Direct Energy entries are one half of the amounts appearing in Table 4, Col. A, "Cost of Purchased Fuels and Electric Energy." The Census data provided no basis for separating Direct Energy (a variable cost) from Indirect Energy (a fixed overhead cost). An arbitrary decision was made to count half of the total energy cost as Direct Energy. The only part of the study this affects is the part in which we estimate the Chinese producer's cost saving derived from pricing based on variable costs only after all overhead has been recovered from sales in China. The energy component is so small that any possible error introduced by considering energy to be half direct and half indirect would not affect the conclusions drawn from this study.

Indirect Labor is found by subtracting Table 2, Col. E, "Production Workers Wages" from Table 2, Col. B, "All Employees Payroll".

Total Cost entries are from Table 2, Col. H, "Total Value of Shipments".

Non-Labor Overhead is found by subtracting Direct Labor, Materials, Direct Energy and Indirect Labor from Total Cost.

The data in Appendix Exhibit B appear in Appendix Exhibit C in percentage form. The Total Cost entries in Col. 6 of Appendix Exhibit B appears in Col. 6 of Appendix Exhibit C as 100%. The entries in columns 1 through 5 of Appendix Exhibit B appear as percentages of total cost in columns 1 through 5 of Appendix Exhibit C. The data in percentage form are used in this study.

You will notice that two lines have been added to the bottom of Appendix Exhibit C. One is for Averages and the other Weighed Averages. In our study we are estimating the cost of goods manufactured in China expressed as a percentage of the cost of the same goods manufactured in the United States. In the study we estimate Chinese costs as a percentage of manufacturing costs in the United States after allowing for three things that cause Chinese costs to be lower. These three things are: (a) the lower cost of Chinese labor, (2) China's pegging to the undervalued Chinese yuan to the United States dollar, and (3) Chinese use of pricing based on variable costs only after overhead costs have been fully recovered from sales in China.

Appendix Exhibit C (Same as text Exhibit 3)
MANUFACTURING COST AS PERCENT OF TOTAL
DOLLAR COST OF GOODS PRODUCED IN THE UNITED
STATES FOR SELECTED INDUSTRY GROUPS

	1	2	3	4	5	6
Industry Groups NAICS Code	Direct Labor	Materials	Direct Energy	Indirect Labor	Non-Labor Overhead	Total Cost
311	6.31	57.31	0.86	3.34	32.18	100.00
312	2.87	35.09	0.36	3.04	58.64	100.00
313	12.77	57.60	1.88	4.83	22.72	100.00
314	10.63	59.98	0.71	5.17	23.51	100.00
315	10.88	53.58	0.33	5.98	29.23	100.00
316	10.68	52.09	0.50	6.11	30.62	100.00
321	12.76	61.65	0.99	4.93	19.67	100.00
322	9.64	43.15	2.34	4.60	30.27	100.00
323	16.81	39.77	0.63	10.13	32.66	100.00
324	1.67	77.96	1.76	1.05	17.56	100.00
325	4.67	48.16	1.86	5.32	39.99	100.00
326	12.70	48.98	1.18	6.35	30.79	100.00
327	13.23	43.69	2.63	5.89	34.56	100.00
331	11.56	60.26	3.15	4.49	20.54	100.00
332	14.97	44.83	0.88	8.56	30.76	100.00
333	10.28	49.83	0.42	9.54	29.93	100.00
334	6.14	47.19	0.31	11.82	34.54	100.00
335	9.79	50.09	0.50	7.28	32.34	100.00
336	6.42	46.69	0.26	3.60	43.03	100.00
337	15.53	44.65	0.50	7.96	31.36	100.00
339	10.39	38.73	0.41	11.11	39.36	100.00
Averages	10.03	51.02	1.07	6.24	31.63	100.00
Wtd. Avg.	9.42	47.82	0.57	9.01	33.18	100.00

The United States imports goods from China in all of the industry group categories listed in Appendix Exhibit C. If the value of goods imported from China were the same for each of these industry groups, then at the bottom of Appendix Exhibit C we would need only a line for averages and would not need the line for weighted averages. However, because there is a great deal of variation in imports from China by industry group, we need to weight the data for volume of imports by category in order to have realistic averages of manufacturing costs of goods imported from China. For this weighting we use the 2004 values of United States imports from China. These imports are shown in Appendix Exhibit D along with the weighting index used to calculate the weighted averages line shown at the bottom of Appendix Exhibit C. In constructing the weighting index the total value of imports is considered to be 1.00 and the index entry for each of the industry groups is calculated by dividing the value for the group by the total value for all industry groups. The weighting index entries are shown in Appendix Exhibit D rounded to three decimal places. However, the weighting index data in the computer, used in applying these data, are not rounded to three decimal places.

Appendix Exhibit D
INDEX FOR COMPUTING WEIGHTED AVERAGE MFG.
COSTS FOR SELECTED INDUSTRY GROUPS, BASED ON
DOLLAR VOLUME OF US IMPORTS FROM CHINA IN THE
YEAR 2004

NAICS Code	Industry Groups	2004 Value of Imports ($1,000's)	Weighting Index
311	Food and Kindred Products	1,280,416	0.007
312	Beverages & Tobacco Prod.	31,911	0.000
313	Textiles and Fabrics	666,382	0.003
314	Textile Mill Products	4,412,749	0.023
315	Apparel & Accessories	13,106,398	0.068
316	Leather & Allied Products	15,442,048	0.081
321	Wood Products	1,821,816	0.010
322	Paper	1,360,325	0.007
323	Printed Matter & Related Prod.	1,414,408	0.007
324	Petroleum & Coal Products	228,053	0.001
325	Chemicals	3,380,551	0.018
326	Plastics & Rubber Products	5,028,421	0.026
327	Nonmetallic Mineral Products	3,419,077	0.018
331	Primary Metal Mfg.	3,049,775	0.016
332	Fabricated Metal Prod. Nesoi	7,549,630	0.039
333	Machinery, Except Electrical	11,169,237	0.058
334	Computer & Electronic Prod.	63,905,745	0.333
335	Elec. Eq. Appliances, Cmpnts	14,735,357	0.077
336	Transportation Equipment	4,144,778	0.022
337	Furniture & Fixtures	10,440,144	0.054
339	Misc. Mfg. Commodities	25,066,309	0.131
	Totals	191,653,530	1.000

Appendix Exhibit E shows for each industry group all of the entries (Columns 1 through 6) multiplied by the corresponding weighting index value. The sums of the columns at the bottom of Appendix Exhibit E comprise the weighted averages line at the bottom of Appendix Exhibit C. For every exhibit in this study for which weighted averages are shown, this procedure is used.

Appendix Exhibit E
CALCULATION OF WEIGHTED AVERAGES FOR
MANUFACTURING COST DATA PRESENTED IN
APPENDIX EXHIBIT C

	1	2	3	4	5	6
Industry Groups NAICS Code	Direct Labor	Materials	Direct Energy	Indirect Labor	Non-Labor Overhead	Total Cost
311	0.04	0.83	0.01	0.02	0.21	0.67
312	0.00	0.01	0.00	0.00	0.01	0.02
313	0.04	0.20	0.01	0.02	0.08	0.35
314	0.24	1.38	0.02	0.12	0.54	2.30
315	0.74	3.66	0.02	0.41	2.00	6.84
316	0.86	4.20	0.04	0.49	2.47	8.06
321	0.12	0.59	0.01	0.05	0.19	0.95
322	0.07	0.38	0.02	0.03	0.21	0.71
323	0.12	0.29	0.00	0.07	0.24	0.74
324	0.00	0.09	0.00	0.00	0.02	0.12
325	0.08	0.85	0.03	0.09	0.71	1.76
326	0.33	1.29	0.03	0.17	0.81	2.62
327	0.24	0.78	0.05	0.11	0.62	1.78
331	0.18	0.96	0.05	0.07	0.33	1.59
332	0.59	1.77	0.03	0.34	1.21	3.94
333	0.60	2.90	0.02	0.56	1.74	5.83
334	2.05	15.74	0.10	3.94	11.52	33.34
335	0.75	3.85	0.04	0.56	2.49	7.69
336	0.14	1,01	0.01	0.08	0.93	2.16
337	0.85	2.43	0.03	0.43	1.71	5.45
339	1.36	5.07	0.05	1.45	5.15	13.08
Totals	9.42	47.82	0.57	9.01	33.18	100.00

This Totals line is the calculated Weighted Averages line that is shown at the bottom of Appendix Exhibit C.

Notes

1. Laura LaHaye, "Mercantilism," *The Concise Encyclopedia of Economics: Library of Economics and Liberty*, November, 2004 (March 7, 2005) <http://www.econlib.org/library/Ecn/Mercantilism.html>
2. For a detailed explanation of the theory of comparative advantage see: Steven Suranovic, "The Theory of Comparative Advantage - Overview," *International Trade Theory and Policy*, August 2, 2003 (October 8, 2003) <http://internationalecon.com/v1.0/ch40/40c000.html#torrens>
3. Laura LaHaye
4. Alan Tonelson, *Race to the Bottom*, (Boulder Colorado, Westview Press, 2002) p.3
5. Ralph Nader, "Introduction: Free Trade and the Decline of Democracy," *The Case Against Free Trade*, (San Francisco, Earth Island Press, 1993) pp. 1-14
6. Table No. 1378. Reserve Assets and International Transaction Balances by Country: 1995 to 2002, *Statistical Abstracts of the United States: 2003*, U.S. Census Bureau (March 7,2005) <http://www.census.gov/prod/2004pubs/03statab/intlstat.pdf>
7. Michael W. Hodges, "Foreign Trade and International Debt Report," *Grandfather Economic*

Reports, August, 2004 (October 10,2004) <httjp://mwhodges.home.att.net/reserves_a.htm>

8. Michael W. Hodges

9. Lou Dobbs, "Coming Up Empty," U.S. *News and World Report*, January 26, 2004, p. 46.

10. "NAM Demands Aggressive Response to Hemorrhage of Manufacturing Jobs," *NAM Online*, October 3, 2003 (February 10, 2004) <http://www.nam.org/tertiary.asp?TrackID=&Cate goryiID=746&DocumentID=27017>

11. News from NAM, "Manufacturing in Crisis: Prospects for Economic Growth," an Address to the Executives Club of Chicago September 30, 2003. *NAM Online*, October 3, 2003 (February 10, 2004) <http://www.nam.org/tertiary.asp?TrackID= &CategoryID=1458DocumentID=27170>

12. Martin Weiss, "Economic Impotence in Washington," *Safe Money Newsletter*, Weiss Research, Inc., Jupiter, Florida, October 4, 2003.

13. Alan Tonelson, p.69.

14. Jodie T. Allen, "Making More Than Money," U.S. *News and World Report*, October 4, 2004, p. 42.

15. Alan Tonelson, p. 81.

16. "U.S. Commodity Trade with 80 Largest U.S. Trading Partners, 1999 to 2003," Industry, Trade, and the Economy: Data and Analysis; International Trade Administration (ITA), U.S. Department of Commerce, *Export.gov*, August 14, 2004 (March 7, 2005) <http://www.ita.doc.gov/td/industry/otea/ usfth/top80cty.html>

17. Neil George, Editor, *Personal Finance*, Volume XXXI, Number 2, January 28, 2004, p. 5.

18. Jayanthi Iyengar, "Radio Tags for China's Products, Blood and People," *Asia Times Online*, August 14, 2004 (August 30, 2004) <www.atimes.com/atimes/china/FH14Ado2.html>

19. "U.S. Companies Urged to Adjust to World Changes," *China View*, September 27, 2004 (October 30, 2004) <www.chinaview.cn>

20. Daniel Denning, "China's Deliberate Economic Attack on America," *Porter Stanberry's News Letter*, Pirate Investor, LLC, Baltimore, MD, March 3, 2004.

21. Elaine Kurtenbach, Associated Press, "GM to Build Cadillacs in China," *The Birmingham News*, November 5, 2003, Sec. D, p. 1.

22. Matthew Benjamin, "China Conundrum," U.S. *News and World Report*, September 15, 2003, p. 37.

23. "United States China Business Council," *China Unique* (March 15, 2005) <http://chinaunique.com/business/bus_coun.htm>

24. "An Introduction and Guide to Staff and Services," Web Site of The United States China Business Council. <http://www.uschina.org/us-china-brochure-final.pdf>

25. "Effects and Consequences of an Emerging China," Testimony of Robert A. Kapp, President, US-China Business Council, before Subcommittee on East Asia and Pacific Affairs, Senate Foreign Relations Committee, March 19, 2003.

<http://foreign.senate.gov/testimony/2003/KappTe
stimony030319.pdf>

26. "U.S. Trade in Goods and Services - Balance of Payments (BOP) Basis, 1960 thru 2004," U.S. Census Bureau, Foreign Trade Statistics, March 11, 2005 (March 15, 2005) <http://www.census.gov/foreign-trade/statistics/historical/gands.pdf.>

27. "Trade (Imports, Exports and Trade Balance) with China: 1985-2005," U.S. Census Bureau Foreign Trade Statistics (March 15, 2005) <http://www.census.gov/foreign-trade/balance/c5700.html#2003>

28. News from NAM

29. "U.S. Imports of All 3-digit NAICS Products with China as of December 2004." U.S. Census Bureau Foreign Trade Statistics <http://www.census.gov/foreign—trade/statistics/product/naics/ctrynaics/i5700_3.html>

30. Paul Andrews, "Courting China," U.S. *News and World Report*, November 24, 2003, p.44.

31. Hennock

32. "Supachai: Sluggish Trade Growth Calls for Urgent Pick Up of Stalled Trade Talks," *World Trade Organization Online*, November 5, 2003, <www.wto.org/english/news_e/pres03_e/pr363_e.htm>

33. Benjamin, p. 37

34. Mary Hennock, BBC News Online Business Reporter, "China: the World's Factory Floor," *BBC News*, November 11, 2002 (March 15, 2005) <http://news.bbc.co.uk/2/hi/business/2415241.stm>

35. Associated Press, "Steel Mill Ticketed for China, in Pieces," *The Birmingham News*, August 26, 2003. Sec. F, p. 1.

36. Laura LaHaye

37. Olivier de Boysson, "Emerging Countries: the Deceptive Simplicity of Floating Currencies," *Conjuncture*, November, 1999, p. 9. <http://economic-research.bnpparibas.com/applis/www/RechEco.nsf/0/76ABF113956C8691C12568 3200373B18/$File/C9911_A2.pdf?OpenElement>

38. Justin Lahart, "Only the Weak Survive," *CNNMoney*, May 20,2003 (March 15, 2005) <http://money.cnn.com/2003/05/markets/competiti vedevaluation>

39. For selected industry groups the percentages of total manufacturing cost shown in Exhibit 3 are derived from Statistics for Industry Groups and Industries: 2001, Annual Survey of Manufacturers, Tables 2 and 4, Census Bureau, U.S. Department of Commerce. The entries in Tables 2 and 4 are in dollar amounts. For additional information on the data used from these tables and on the procedures followed see the Mathematical Appendix.

40. Lou Dobbs, p. 46

41. "NAM Letter to Snow on Unemployment and the Chinese Currency," *NAM Online*, October 3, 2003 (March 15,2005) <http://www.nam.org/tertiary. asp?TrackID=&categoryID=1&DocumentID=2682 9>

42. "Pressure Mounts on China's Yuan," *BBC Business News Online*, August 28, 2003 (March

Organizations Desiring

SPECIAL DISCOUNTS FOR QUANTITY PURCHASES

Contact

Bookman Publishing & Marketing
35 Industrial Drive, Suite 104
Martinsville, IN 46151

Or Call: 800-342-6068

Or FAX: 765-342-7217